Lulu and Bell

Published by Lulu and Bell
ISBN: 978-1-83990-103-4
Lulu and Bell 2021

Contents

Start the day positively	1 – 6
Write it down	7 – 8
How to lift your mood	9 – 13
Walk your own path	14 – 17
Create a visual mood board	18 – 19
Affirmations	20 – 22
What did you say?	23 – 24
Gratitude	25 – 27
Move out of your comfort zone	28 – 30

Imaginary shield	31 - 33
This is me	34 - 36
It's ok to make mistakes	37 - 38
Just getting started	39 - 40

Start the day positively

How you start your morning can have a large impact on the rest of your day, starting it in a positive manner can influence how your day goes.

How you start your morning can change your whole day.

Creating a morning routine encourages positive habits, helps you to embrace your day and puts you in a good frame of mind.

Positive changes you can make to your morning

01. **Set your alarm:** Wake up with enough time, to get everything done that you need to and are not rushing.

02. **Remove your phone** from your bedroom, so it isn't the first thing that you look for, charge it in a different room, so it can't distract you.

Challenge: Try not to look at your phone for the first hour after you wake up.

03. **Journaling:** Write down what you want to achieve that day, write a list of things you need to do and goals you want to achieve. List some affirmations.

04. **Get moving:** Set your alarm half an hour early and do some exercise, go for a run, a walk, yoga, stretching or just put on some music and dance around the kitchen.

Get those endorphins moving

05. **Meditation/breathwork:** Taking 5 or 10 minutes in the morning to do some meditation can really help to calm the mind and relax the body. There are several meditation videos online and free apps that you can use. A very simple breathing exercise that you can try is:

> Breathe in for 4 counts
> Hold for 4 counts
> Breathe out for 5 counts

Morning Routine

Write down your new morning routine

Write it down

Journaling is a great way to learn more about yourself, helping you to process your different feelings and thoughts. It also can help with relieving stress and building confidence.

Putting your thoughts on paper, can help you to clear your mind and gain a different perspective.

It can help improve your mood, well-being and happiness. So what are you waiting for, get creative and start expressing yourself.

Journal prompts

- List five things which bring you the most happiness?

- What was your favourite thing about today?

- How can you make tomorrow the best day?

- What makes you laugh?

- What makes you smile?

- What is your biggest dream?

How to lift your mood

Some days you can find yourself feeling low. It may be because of someone else, something that has happened that day or you have just woken up not feeling yourself.

Dong something you enjoy or that will make you feel better can really help switch your mood. For some people this could be watching a funny movie or going for a run. Having a list of activites you can turn to which you know will make you feel better can really help with lifting your mood.

Every day may not be good but there is something good in every day.

Here are some suggestions of feel good activities you can try.

01. Listen to music

List the songs that make you feel empowered, happy or strong. (Now put that song on and sing those lyrics!)

_____   _____

_____   _____

_____   _____

_____   _____

02. Get moving! Dance like no one is watching, go for a run, get your body moving.

03. Take a walk in nature.

IMPORTANT!

04. Watch something funny.

05. Get creative, start drawing, painting, express yourself.

Do more of what makes you happy.

List the different activities that lift your mood.

01. _____

02. _____

03. _____

04. _____

05. _____

Life is not about waiting for the storm to pass it's about learning to dance in the rain.

Quote by Vivian Greene

Walk your own path

Have you ever found yourself scrolling through social media and comparing yourself and your life to others. I know I have, and it made me feel pretty miserable. We should never compare ourselves to other people, we are all unique. So lets focus on ourselves, our dreams and goals and don't worry what other people are doing, this is your life and there is only one of you and this is what makes you so special.

Happiness is found when you stop comparing yourself to other people.

Focus on you

- Have a no social media day, where you don't go on any social media all day or if you find this difficult initially, set a timer and only allow yourself 30 mins.

- Start looking at the accounts that you are following and how they make you feel, unfollow accounts which tend to not make you feel good.

- Be aware of what you are feeding your brain. Read books, magazines, listen to podcasts and music that is inspiring, motivational and empowering, that lifts you and makes you feel amazing.

- Write down your strengths, talents and accomplishments. If you find this difficult, ask a friend or family member for their opinion.

Accomplishments

Strengthens

Talents

YOU GOT THIS!

If you find this task difficult, think about what you would like to accomplish or what new skills you would like to try.

YOUR UNIQUENESS IS YOUR MAGIC

Create a visual mood board

Creating a visual mood board with your dreams and goals can really help you stay focused on what you want to achieve in your life. Also by putting inspiring quotes and affirmations on your board can also help to lift your mood.

What you need:

- Magazines, print pictures from the internet
- Pinboard, memo board
- Scissors
- Pens, pencils, paper
- Pins/clips

Remember to put your board in a place you will look at every day

Dream Big

Affirmations

Affirmations are positive words and sentences, which help with creating more positive self talk and thoughts. Using affirmations can create a stronger mental attitude, build our self esteem and lift our moods.

Become your own cheerleader

Some examples of affirmations

My confidence increases every day

I am worthy

I believe in myself and my abilities

I love life

I am beautiful

Create your own affirmations

01.

02.

03.

04.

05.

Every morning look in the mirror and repeat these affirmations to yourself.

What did you say?

Often we can become our own worst critic, telling ourselves we are useless or unworthy. This type of negative self-talk can have a large effect on our self-esteem and make us feel negative about ourselves.

Next time this negative self-talk enters your mind or you hear yourself talking about yourself negatively. STOP and THINK. Would you talk to a friend or even a stranger in this way, what evidence do you have to back up this statement?

Try putting a positive spin on the negative talk and use affirmations to counteract it.

Remember be kind to yourself

Think about any negative self-talk you have had previously and flip them into positives, now write these positive statements in the hearts.

Gratitude

Practising gratitude can help you to focus on the positive elements within your life, allowing you to focus on what is important and finding the moments to be grateful for. Keeping a gratitude journal to write down every day what you are grateful for can help you to express gratitude.

Rather than focusing on what you don't have, focus on what you do have.

This is a good activity to do just before you go to bed at night.

What are you grateful for.

01.

02.

03.

04.

05.

Do more of what makes you happy

Move out of your comfort zone

To help us grow as a person and build our confidence, it is important at times to step out of our comfort zone and do something that scares us a little. This could be delivering a presentation, trying a new hobby or meeting new people. It may feel scary initially but the more often we step out of our comfort zone the less scary it will be. By stepping out of our comfort zone, it helps us to learn and develop as a person and therefore grow.

Try ~ otherwise you will never know.

01.

02.

Write down an activity you could do each week that would take you out of your comfort zone.

03.

04.

Imaginary shield

Sometimes we can feel as if we are carrying all our worries and fears around with us. This can make us feel anxious and lower mood. Having techniques and activities to help lessen our load can really help with making us feel better and lighter.

Here are some activities you can try:

- Write down all your worries and fears on a piece of paper. Once you have done this, rip the paper into several pieces and place it in a bin. This activity symbolises that you are now letting go of these worries and fears and they don't belong in your life anymore.

- Meditation has several benefits. It can help with reducing negative thoughts, manage stress and help with becoming more self-aware. It can help make you feel less anxious and make you feel calmer and relaxed.

 The following meditation can help you feel protected, helping you to create an imaginary shield around you to protect you from outside worries and fears.

Sit or lie in a comfortable position, away from any distractions or noise.
And close your eyes.
Take a deep breath in, and then exhale, breathing out any worries or fears.
Do this twice more.
Now that your body and mind are relaxed,
I want you to imagine a magical shield around you, protecting you.
I want you to visualize this shield.
Now I want you to imagine any worries or fears you have bouncing off this shield, and disappearing into the air.
Take a moment to visualize this.
Then I want you to imagine your shield shining a bright light all around you, protecting you and keeping you safe.
Take a moment to visualize this.
Then when you are ready you can open your eyes

DON'T FORGET

You've got this

This is me

We are all amazing human beings, who are unique and special. We are not going to be liked by everyone, and some people will only like you if you fit into their box but you shouldn't feel the need to change yourself to fit in. Believe in yourself, be you and don't apologise for it.

> Don't dim your light because someone didn't like how bright it was shining.

It's ok to make mistakes

We have all made mistakes in our life and this is ok. Mistakes are how we learn and grow as people. Mistakes can build are resilience and help us to explore alternatives. It takes bravery to admit our mistakes, learn from them and move on.

List some of the mistakes you have made in life and what you have learnt from them.

THINK OF THE MISTAKES YOU MAKE AS PROGRESSION

Just getting started

The journey doesn't end here, this is just the start of your self-love journey. Continue the activities in this book, buy yourself a journal and make yourself a priority. Keep checking back at the progress you are making and be proud of yourself.

TO DO

Make yourself a priority

www.ingramcontent.com/pod-product-compliance
Lightning Source LLC
Chambersburg PA
CBHW051254110526
44588CB00026B/2994